Bond

Maths

Assessment Papers

6-7 years

OXFORD
UNIVERSITY PRESS

OXFORD
UNIVERSITY PRESS

Great Clarendon Street, Oxford, OX2 6DP, United Kingdom

Oxford University Press is a department of the University of Oxford.
It furthers the University's objective of excellence in research,
scholarship, and education by publishing worldwide. Oxford is
a registered trade mark of Oxford University Press in the UK and in
certain other countries

British Library Cataloguing in Publication Data
Data available

978-0-19-274011-3

10 9 8 7 6 5 4 3 2

Paper used in the production of this book is a natural, recyclable
product made from wood grown in sustainable forests.
The manufacturing process conforms to the environmental
regulations of the country of origin.

Printed in China

Acknowledgements

The publishers would like to thank the following for permissions to
use copyright material:

Illustrations: Russell Parry
Page make-up: Tech-Set Ltd
Cover illustrations: Lo Cole

Although we have made every effort to trace and contact all
copyright holders before publication this has not been possible in all
cases. If notified, the publisher will rectify any errors or omissions at
the earliest opportunity.

Links to third party websites are provided by Oxford in good faith
and for information only. Oxford disclaims any responsibility for
the materials contained in any third party website referenced in
this work.

Before you get started

What is Bond?

This book is part of the Bond Assessment Papers series for maths, which provides **thorough and continuous practice of all the key maths content** from ages five to thirteen. Bond's maths resources are ideal preparation for many different kinds of tests and exams – from SATs to 11+ and other secondary school selection exams.

What does this book cover?

It covers all the maths that a child of this age would be expected to learn and is fully in line with the National Curriculum for maths and the National Numeracy Strategy. One of the key features of Bond Assessment Papers is that each one practises **a wide variety of skills and question types** so that children are always challenged to think – and don't get bored repeating the same question type again and again. We think that variety is the key to effective learning. It helps children 'think on their feet' and cope with the unexpected.

The age given on the cover is for guidance only. As the papers are designed to be reasonably challenging for the age group, any one child may naturally find him or herself working above or below the stated age. The important thing is that children are always encouraged by their performance. Working at the right level is the key to this.

What does the book contain?

- **20 papers** – each one contains 25 questions.
- **Scoring devices** – there are score boxes in the margins and a Progress Chart on page 44. The chart is a visual and motivating way for children to see how they are doing. Encouraging them to colour in the chart as they go along and to try to beat their last score can be highly effective!
- **Next Steps** – advice on what to do after finishing the papers can be found on the inside back cover.
- **Answers** – located in an easily-removed central pull-out section.
- **Key maths words** – on page 1 you will find a glossary of special key words that are used in the papers. These are highlighted in bold each time that they appear. These words are now used in the maths curriculum and children are expected to know them at this age.

How can you use this book?

One of the great strengths of Bond Assessment Papers is their flexibility. They can be used at home, school and by tutors to:

- provide regular maths practice in **bite-sized chunks**
- **highlight strengths and weaknesses** in the core skills

- identify **individual needs**
- set **homework**
- set **timed formal practice** tests – allow about 25 minutes.

It is best to start at the beginning and work though the papers in order.

What does a score mean and how can it be improved?

If children colour in the Progress Chart at the back, this will give you an idea of how they are doing. The Next Steps inside the back cover will help you to decide what to do next to help a child progress. We suggest that it is always valuable to go over any wrong answers with children.

Don't forget the website...!

Visit www.bond11plus.co.uk for lots of advice, information and suggestions on everything to do with Bond, exams, and helping children to do their best.

Key words

Some special maths words are used in this book. You will find them in **bold** each time they appear in the papers. These words are explained here.

anticlockwise	the opposite direction to which the hands of a clock turn
calculation	working with numbers to find an answer
clockwise	the direction that the hands of a clock turn
digit	a digit is part of a number. Some numbers can be written with just one digit: e.g. 5 has one digit, 84 has two, 512 has three
double	the answer when a number is multiplied by 2
estimate	a sensible 'guess' at the position of a number on a number line or at the quantity of objects in a set
even numbers	whole numbers that can be divided exactly by two: 2, 4, 6, 8 are even numbers
figures	another name for numbers: e.g. 9 rather than 'nine'
fraction	a part of a whole, written like this: $\frac{1}{2}$ $\frac{1}{4}$ $\frac{2}{3}$ $\frac{2}{3}$ means two parts out of three equal parts
half	the answer when a number is divided by 2
halve	the answer when a number is divided by 2
hexagon	a 2D (flat) shape with six straight sides
line of symmetry	the line on which a mirror can be placed to show the reflection of a shape
missing number	numbers that are omitted from a sequence or a calculation: often represented with a box
multiple	a number which another number multiplies into: 5, 10, 15, 20, 50, 75, 135, 200 are all multiples of 5
odd numbers	whole numbers that cannot be divided exactly by two: 1, 3, 5, 7, 9 are odd numbers
pentagon	a 2D (flat) shape with five straight sides
quadrilateral	a 2D (flat) shape with four straight sides
right angle	an angle that is equal to one quarter of a whole turn
round	round means roughly or approximately: 54 rounded to the nearest 10 is 50 26 rounded to the nearest 10 is 30
sequence	a set of numbers, shapes or quantities placed in an order according to a rule
set	a collection of numbers, shapes or quantities
sum	the answer when two or more numbers are added together
symmetry	a shape has symmetry if it has one or more lines of symmetry, like this
Venn diagram	a chart for sorting information of different kinds

Paper 1

Write in the **missing number** names in each **sequence**.

1 seventeen, eighteen, nineteen, _twenty_ .

2–3 _twenty_, thirty, thirty-one, _thirty two_ .
twnine

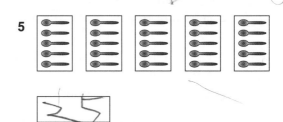
Thirty two

How many spoons?

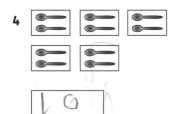

4 ▢ 10

5 ▢ 25

6–8 The number square has a hole.

What are the three **missing numbers**?

Write them on the grid.

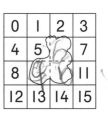

Write in the answers.

9 3 + 2 = ▢ 5

10 1 + 4 = ▢ 5

11 4 + 3 = ▢ 7

12 5 + 0 = ▢ 5

13 2 + 2 = ▢ 4

14–16 What time is it? Write the time under each clock.

_____   _____   _____

Write in the **missing numbers**.

17 1 more than 39 is ▢

18 1 more than 100 is ▢

(2)

Ring the name of each shape.

19

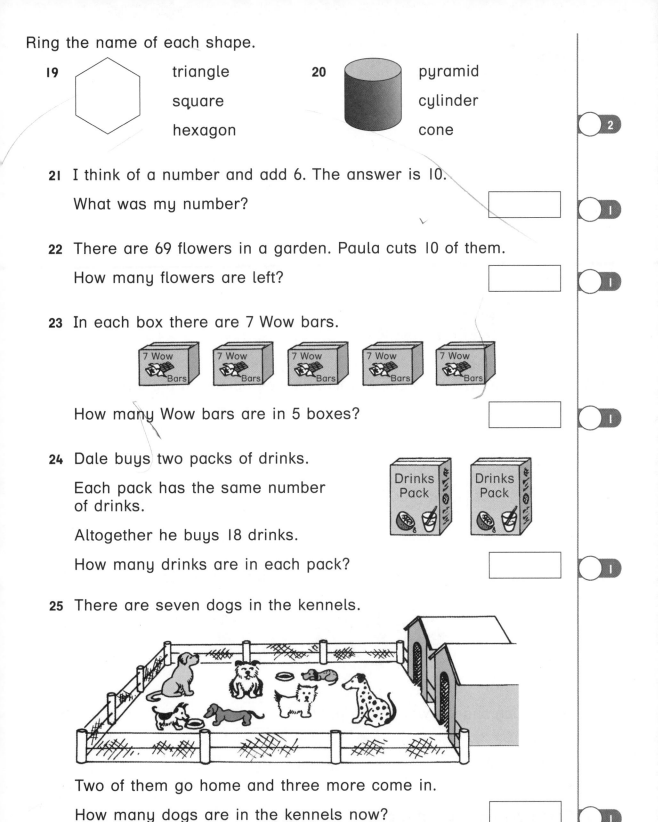

triangle

square

hexagon

20

pyramid

cylinder

cone

2

21 I think of a number and add 6. The answer is 10.

What was my number?

1

22 There are 69 flowers in a garden. Paula cuts 10 of them.

How many flowers are left?

1

23 In each box there are 7 Wow bars.

How many Wow bars are in 5 boxes?

1

24 Dale buys two packs of drinks.

Each pack has the same number of drinks.

Altogether he buys 18 drinks.

How many drinks are in each pack?

1

25 There are seven dogs in the kennels.

Two of them go home and three more come in.

How many dogs are in the kennels now?

1

How many apples?

1   2

[ ]   [ ]   2

How many pears?

3    [ ]   1

4–6 Draw more arrows to show which shapes belong in the **set**.

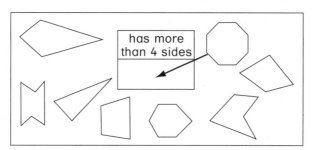

has more than 4 sides

                                                        3

7–8 Ring the coin or coins you could use to buy the apple.

 9p

How much change would you get? [ ] p   2

9 double 3 = [ ]   **10 half** of 8 = [ ]   2

11 Sam eats one **half** of a bar of chocolate.

What **fraction** of the whole bar is left? [ ]   1

Match the number names to the correct **figures**.

12–15

twenty-five   52
two hundred and five ——————— 20
twenty ——   25
fifty-two   520
five hundred and twenty   205

  4

Write the numbers in order, smallest first.

16   39   82   75   46   93

[ ]   [ ]   [ ]   [ ]   [ ]

17   307   703   730   370   303

[ ]   [ ]   [ ]   [ ]   [ ]

  2

Here are five number cards. | 4 | 7 | 5 | 2 | 0 |

18 Use two of the cards to make
    a number more than 70.   [|]

19 Use two of the cards to make
    a number greater than 10/less than 30.   [|]

20 Use two of the cards to make
    a number between 40 and 50.   [|]

21 Use three of the cards to make
    a number more than 750.   [| |]

22 Use three of the cards to make
    the number halfway between 400 and 450.   [| |]

  5

Write in the **missing number**.

23 682 = [   ] + 80 + 2

24 950 = 900 + 50 + [   ]

25 3 hundreds + 4 tens + 9 units = [   ]

 3

Now go to the Progress Chart to record your score!   Total   25

5

Paper 3

Write in the answers.

1 2 − 1 = ☐

2 4 − 2 = ☐

3 5 − 4 = ☐

4 5 − 3 = ☐

5 3 − 0 = ☐

Write in the **missing number**.

6 1 less than 80 is ☐

7 1 less than 101 is ☐

8 Put rings around three numbers to make 16.

1	2	3	4	5
6	7	8	9	10

Number of cars in families of Year 2 children ☺ = 1 family

3 cars | ☺ ☺ ☺
2 cars | ☺ ☺ ☺ ☺ ☺ ☺
1 car | ☺ ☺ ☺ ☺ ☺ ☺ ☺ ☺ ☺ ☺ ☺ ☺ ☺
0 cars | ☺ ☺ ☺ ☺ ☺ ☺ ☺ ☺

Every child belongs to a different family.

9 How many families do not have a car?

10 How many families own one car?

11 How many more families have two cars than have three cars?

12 How many children are in Year 2?

13 How many cars are owned by families of children in Year 2?

Write in the answers.

14 12 + 8 = ☐   **15** 17 + 3 = ☐

16 9 + 11 = ☐   **17** 4 + 4 = ☐

18 8 + 8 = ☐   **19** 10 + 10 = ☐

◯ 6

 17p

20 Tick the coins for the correct amount needed to buy the can.

◯ 1

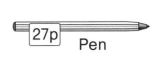 27p Pen

 Notebook 30p

 21p Pencil

 18p Rubber

21 Ario buys a pen and a pencil.
How much do they cost him altogether? ☐

22 Emma buys a rubber with a 20p coin.
How much change should she get? ☐

23 Leon buys 5 rubbers. How much does he spend? ☐

24 Jodie buys a notebook using only 5p coins.
How many 5p coins did she use? ☐

25 Dino uses two 20p coins and a 5p coin
to buy two items and has no change.

Ring the two items he buys.

◯ 5

  Notebook

Write in the **missing numbers** in each **sequence**.

1-2

	20	30	40	50	

3-5

101	111	121	131			

5

What position is each shape in the pattern?

Example The first white square is *fourth*.

6 The third circle is _____ .

7 The first white triangle is _____ .

8 The second white square is _____ .

3

Write the time shown under each clock.

9

_____

10

_____

2

Write in the **missing number**.

11 10 more than 39 is [ ]

12 10 more than 190 is [ ]

13 10 more than 493 is [ ]

3

This is a pizza cut into four equal pieces.

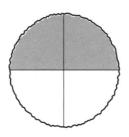

14 How many quarters of the pizza are shaded?

15 How many halves of the pizza are shaded?

16 How many quarters of the pizza are not shaded? 3

17 Ring the shortest length.

    81 m   18 m   39 m   93 m   38 m

18 Ring the longest length.

    217 cm   172 cm   271 cm   721 cm   127 cm   2

Write in the **missing numbers**.

19 $271 = 70 + 1 +$ ☐

20 $394 =$ ☐ hundreds, 9 tens and 4 units

21 5 hundreds and 7 units $=$ ☐   3

Write in the **missing numbers**.

22 $9 + 3 = 6 +$ ☐

23 $32 + 10 = 12 +$ ☐

24 $9 - 6 = 7 -$ ☐

25 $15 - 4 = 20 -$ ☐   4

Paper 5

Write in the answers.

1 31 − 19 = ☐   **2** 53 − 48 = ☐   2

What is the answer?

3 two fives   ☐

4 5 multiplied by 10   ☐

5 multiply 8 by 2   ☐   3

Jill sorts names of colours.

3 letters	4 letters	5 letters	6 letters	more than 6 letters
red	grey blue pink	green brown mauve white	yellow orange purple	turquoise magenta

6 How many of the colours have exactly 6 letters?   ☐

7 How many of the colours have fewer than 6 letters?   ☐

8 Which two groups have the same number of colours?   ☐ and ☐

9 How many colours did Jill sort altogether?   ☐

10 Write the colour name 'black' in the correct place on the chart.   5

Ring the addition that has a different answer to the other four.

11 4 + 4   2 + 6   1 + 7   5 + 3   6 + 3

12 1 + 8   7 + 2   5 + 4   7 + 3   3 + 6

13 2 + 5   4 + 3   5 + 2   6 + 1   9 + 0

14 | 5 + 5 | | 2 + 8 | | 3 + 7 | | 6 + 2 | | 4 + 6 |

15 | 4 + 8 | | 5 + 7 | | 8 + 2 | | 6 + 6 | | 7 + 5 | ◯ 5

16 Simon started for school at 8:30. He got there 15 minutes later.

At what time did he get to school?

17 Claire is 120 cm tall. Her mum is 160 cm tall.

How much shorter is Claire than her mum?

18 To bake a cake Jade needs 25 g of mixed peel.

How many grams does she need for two cakes?

19 Justine shares a one litre bottle of juice equally between herself and a friend.

How much juice does each get?

20 A plane leaves at 3:00. It is due to arrive at 5:15, but it is 30 minutes late.

At what time does the plane arrive?   ◯ 5

21 Put a ring around the number that cannot be divided exactly by 5.

100   50   65   52   25

22 Put a ring around the number that can be divided exactly by both 2 and 5.

44   15   52   90   25   ◯ 2

23 Write the **odd number** that is less than 17 and more than 13.

24–25 Write two **even numbers** that are between 84 and 90.   [ ] and [ ]   ◯ 3

Paper 6

1 7 + 8 = ◻   **2** 60 + 50 = ◻   ◯ 2

3–5 Draw lines to match each **calculation** to its answer.

| 47 add 12 | add 30 to 8 | 60 plus 20 |

| 28 | 69 | 80 | 38 | 59 |

◯ 3

6 Write these amounts in order, smallest first.

£4   195p   £1.59   40p

◻ ◻ ◻ ◻

◯ 1

7 What day comes six days after a Tuesday?   _____

8 Which letter is the 25th letter of the alphabet?   _____

◯ 2

Put a ring around the correct **missing number**.

9 1 × ◻ = 1   1 2 3 4 5 6 7 8 9 10

10 ◻ × 10 = 60   1 2 3 4 5 6 7 8 9 10

11 9 × ◻ = 90   1 2 3 4 5 6 7 8 9 10

12 ◻ × 1 = 7   1 2 3 4 5 6 7 8 9 10

13 8 × ◻ = 8   1 2 3 4 5 6 7 8 9 10

◯ 5

14 Shade the triangle in the square after the turn.

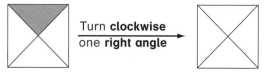

Turn **clockwise** one **right angle**

◯ 1

15 Geri pours another 200 ml into the jug.

How many millilitres are in the jug now?   ◻

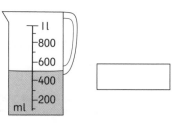

◯ 1

16 Ring two numbers with a **sum** of 90.

30	5	10
20	25	35
15	60	40

17 In three games Javed scores 7, 8 and 3 points.
How many points does he score altogether?

18 I think of a number and subtract 8. The answer is 12.
What was my number?

19 A lorry has 6 wheels.
How many wheels do 10 lorries have?

20 Lucas has 70 books. He puts them into ten equal piles.
How many books are in each pile?

21 Debbie plants ten groups of bulbs. In each group
she plants 5 daffodil bulbs and 6 tulip bulbs.
How many bulbs does she plant altogether?

5

Write in the **missing numbers**.

22 40 — **halve** → ☐ — **double** → ☐

23 26 — **halve** → ☐ — **double** → ☐

24 45 — **double** → ☐ — **halve** → ☐

3

25 **Estimate** the number of small shaded
squares needed to go around the edge
of the rectangle. ☐

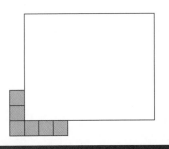

1

Paper 7

Write in the answers.

1   2 + 1 + 3 = ☐

2   1 + 3 + 3 = ☐

3   4 + 2 + 1 = ☐

Write in the answers.

4   **double** 5 = ☐

5   **half** of 16 = ☐

6   7 + 7 = ☐

7   9 + 9 = ☐

What **fraction** of each shape is shaded?

8
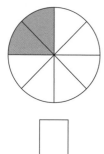
☐

9
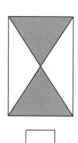
☐

Put rings around the two subtractions that have the same answer.

10 6 − 5	11 − 2	5 − 0	7 − 3	9 − 4
11 6 − 2	9 − 7	18 − 17	14 − 13	7 − 2
12 8 − 1	10 − 8	4 − 0	14 − 8	16 − 9
13 10 − 9	8 − 5	17 − 11	9 − 5	11 − 8
14 10 − 10	9 − 0	19 − 17	12 − 2	15 − 13

Write in the answers.

15   40 + 60 = ☐

16   80 + 20 = ☐

17   10 + 90 = ☐

Round these numbers to the nearest 10.

18 74 to the nearest 10 is ☐

19 157 to the nearest 10 is ☐

Wally and Shahid made a chart of favourite colours.

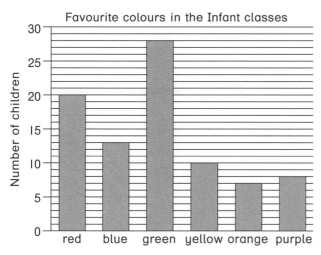

Favourite colours in the Infant classes

20 Which is the favourite colour of the most children? _____

21 Which is the favourite colour of the fewest children? _____

22 How many children like blue the best? ☐

23 How many more children like purple than like orange the best? ☐

24 Which colour is the favourite of twice as many children as like yellow? _____

5

25 Tick four coins to make £2.50.

Paper 8

1–2 There is a hole in the number square.

What are the two **missing numbers**?

Write them on the grid.

36	35	34	33	32	31
30	29	28	27	26	25
24	23	22		20	19
18	17		15	14	13
12	11	10	9	8	7
6	5	4	3	2	1

2

Put a ring around the correct answer.

3 5 × 10 | 10   20   30   40   50   60 |

4 2 × 2 | 2   4   6   8   10   12 |

5 1 × 10 | 10   20   30   40   50   60 |

6 4 × 2 | 2   4   6   8   10   12 |

7 10 × 2 | 10   20   30   40   50   60 |

5

Find the **missing numbers** in each **sequence**.

8–9 | 75 | | 80 | | 85 | | | | 95 | | |

10–12 | | | 109 | | 106 | | 103 | | | | |

5

Draw lines to match each **calculation** to its correct answer.

13–15 | take 30 from 70 | | 27 subtract 3 | | 5 less than 9 |

| 4 | | 59 | | 30 | | 40 | | 24 |

3

16

Times children in Year 2 leave home to come to school

= I child

16 How many children leave home at half-past 8?

17 How many more children leave home at
quarter-past 8 than at 8 o'clock?

18 Nine girls leave home at 8:15.

How many boys leave home at 8:15?

19 James leaves home at 8:45. The school bell rings at 8:50.

Put a ring around the distance you think he lives from school.

100 mm   100 cm   100 m   100 km

20 How many children are in Year 2 altogether?

5

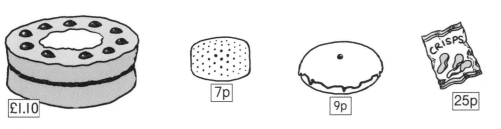

£1.10   7p   9p   25p

21 What is the total cost of a bun and a biscuit?

22 Arthur buys a packet of crisps with a 50p coin.
How much change does he get?

23 Alice buys 10 biscuits.
How much do they cost her altogether?

24 Becky has £1.
What is the greatest number of buns she can buy?

25 Wally wants to buy a cake and some crisps. He has £2.
How many packets of crisps can he buy
as well as a cake?

5

Paper 9

Write in the answers.

1   7 + 6 + 4 = [   ]   2   5 + 9 + 6 = [   ]

3   38 + 9   = [   ]   4   58 − 21   = [   ]

      4

5

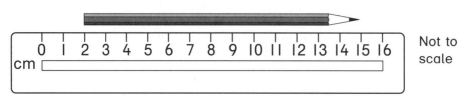

Not to scale

How many centimetres long is the pencil?   [   ]   **1**

Write in the answers.

6   75 + 3   = [   ]   7   400 + 9 = [   ]

8   50 + 36 = [   ]   9   37 + 12 = [   ]

10   64 + 10 = [   ]

      5

Write in the **missing numbers**.

11–12   8 + 9   = [17   ]

         18 + 19 = [   ]

         28 + 29 = [   ]

      2

13   Use a ruler to draw more lines to make a single square, using the existing lines.

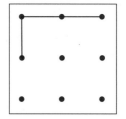

      1

14   If 12 apples are shared equally between 2 children, how many apples is each child given?   [   ]

15   Divide 15 by 5.   [   ]

      2

Write in the answers.

16   **double** 10 is [   ]   17   **half** of 30 is

      2

18 Al has 12 strawberries.

He eats one quarter of them

How many strawberries did he eat?

[ ]

19 Dixie has some swap cards.

She gives a quarter of them to her brother.

What **fraction** of her swap cards does she have left?

[ ] 2

20 Tick the clock with its two hands at a **right angle.**

[ ] 1

Write a subtraction that uses the same numbers as the addition.

21   Addition   Subtraction

$\boxed{26}$ + $\boxed{13}$ = $\boxed{39}$ $\boxed{}$ – $\boxed{}$ = $\boxed{}$

[ ] 1

22–23 Tick the coins needed to buy both the ice-cream and the ice-lolly.

45p 25p

How much change should you get if you
pay with a £1 coin?

[ ] 2

24–25 Three balls balance five bricks.

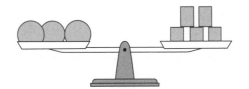

How many bricks will balance 9 balls?

[ ]

How many balls will balance 50 bricks?

[ ] 2

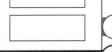

Paper 10

Write in the answers.

1 7 + 7 = [   ]

2 2 + 8 = [   ]

3 6 + 3 = [   ]

4 8 + 1 = [   ]

5 3 + 5 = [   ]

5

This is a table of the number of boys and girls in five families.

Family	Number of girls	Number of boys
Abel	0	3
Ball	2	2
Crew	4	1
Delf	1	1
Foss	2	5

6 Which family has two children? _____

7 Which family has the most children? _____

8 How many fewer boys than girls are in the Crew family? [   ]

9 How many more boys than girls are in the five families? [   ]

10 How many children are there altogether in the five families? [   ]

5

Write in the **missing numbers**.

11 **double** 15 = [   ]

12 **half** of 70 = [   ]

2

Put a ring around the best unit to measure each quantity.

13 A bucketful of water

ml   g   m   l   kg   km

14 The weight of one cherry

ml   g   m   l   kg   km

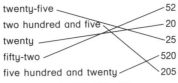

Paper 1

1. twenty
2. twenty-nine
3. thirty-two
4. 10
5. 25

6–8

0	1	2	3
4	5	**6**	7
8	**9**	**10**	11
12	13	14	15

9. 5
10. 5
11. 7
12. 5
13. 4
14. 7 o'clock or 7.00 or 19:00
15. 12 o'clock or 12.00 or noon/midnight or 00:00
16. half-past 4 or 4.30 or 16:30
17. 40
18. 101
19. hexagon
20. cylinder
21. 4   22. 59
23. 35   24. 9
25. 8

Paper 2

1. 16
2. 35
3. 32

4–6

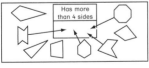
Has more than 4 sides

7. 5p + 5p or 10p
8. 1p
9. 6
10. 4
11. $\frac{1}{2}$

12–15

twenty-five — 52
two hundred and five — 20
twenty — 25
fifty-two — 520
five hundred and twenty — 205

16. 39, 46, 75, 82, 93
17. 303, 307, 370, 703, 730
18. 72 or 74 or 75
19. 20 or 24 or 25 or 27
20. 42 or 45 or 47
21. 752 or 754
22. 425
23. 600
24. 0
25. 349

Paper 3

1. 1   2. 2
3. 1   4. 2
5. 3   6. 79
7. 100
8. *any combination of three numbers which add up to 16*
9. 8   10. 13
11. 3   12. 30
13. 34   14. 20
15. 20   16. 20
17. 8   18. 16
19. 20
20. e.g.

or

e.g.

21. 48p
22. 2p
23. 90p
24. 6
25. Rubber

Pen

Paper 4

1. 10   2. 60
3. 141   4. 151
5. 161   6. ninth
7. eighth   8. seventh
9. half-past 9 or 9.30 or 21:30
10. quarter-past 1 or 1.15 or 13:15
11. 49
12. 200
13. 503
14. 2
15. 1
16. 2
17. 18 m
18. 721 cm
19. 200   20. 3
21. 507   22. 6
23. 30   24. 4
25. 9

Paper 5

1. 12   2. 5
3. 10   4. 50
5. 16   6. 3
7. 8   8. 4, 6
9. 13
10.

3 letters	4 letters	5 letters	6 letters	more than 6 letters
red	grey	green	yellow	turquoise
blue	brown	orange	purple	
pink	mauve	purple		
	white			
	black			

11. 6 + 3   12. 7 + 3
13. 9 + 0   14. 6 + 2
15. 8 + 2   16. quarter to 9 or 8:45
17. 40 cm
18. 50 g
19. $\frac{1}{2}$ litre or 500 ml or 0.5 l
20. 5.45 or quarter to 6
21. 52   22. 90
23. 15   24. 86
25. 88

Paper 6

1 15   **2** 110

3–5

6 40p, £1.59, 195p, £4
7 Monday   **8** y
9 1   **10** 6
11 10   **12** 7
13 1
14

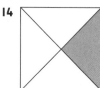

15 700 ml
16

17 18   **18** 20
19 60   **20** 7
21 110   **22** 20, 40
23 13, 26   **24** 90, 45
25 *accept as correct 30 to 40, inclusive*

Paper 7

1 6   **2** 7
3 7   **4** 10
5 8   **6** 14
7 18
8 $\frac{2}{8}$ or $\frac{1}{4}$
9 $\frac{2}{4}$ or $\frac{1}{2}$
10 5 − 0 and 9 − 4
11 18 − 17 and 14 − 13
12 8 − 1 and 16 − 9
13 8 − 5 and 11 − 8
14 19 − 17 and 15 − 13
15 100   **16** 100

17 100   **18** 70
19 160   **20** green
21 orange   **22** 13
23 1   **24** red
25

Paper 8

1–2

36	35	34	33	32	31
30	29	28	27	26	25
24	23	22	**21**	20	19
18	17	**16**	15	14	13
12	11	10	9	8	7
6	5	4	3	2	1

3 50   **4** 4
5 10   **6** 8
7 20   **8** 90
9 100   **10** 112
11 100   **12** 97

13–15

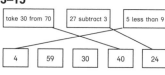

16 6   **17** 4
18 3   **19** 100 m
20 27   **21** 16p
22 25p   **23** 70p
24 11   **25** 3

Paper 9

1 17   **2** 20
3 47   **4** 37
5 13 cm   **6** 78
7 409   **8** 86
9 49   **10** 74
11 37   **12** 57

13

14 6
15 3   **16** 20
17 15   **18** 3
19 $\frac{3}{4}$
20

21 39 − 13 = 26 or
39 − 26 = 13
22

23 30p
24 15
25 30

Paper 10

1 14   **2** 10
3 9   **4** 9
5 8   **6** Delf
7 Foss   **8** 3
9 3   **10** 21
11 30   **12** 35
13 l   **14** g
15 m   **16** + =
17 − =   **18** 200 cm
or = +   or 2 m
19 1925 g   **20** 1250 ml
21 12 min
22 100 cm or 1 m
23 80
24 86
25 17

Paper 11

1 8   **2** 3
3 5   **4** 2
5 6

6 accept line between 12.8 and 13.2 cm

7 7 × 2   **8** 9 × 10

9 3 × 2   **10** 2 × 10

11 3 × 10   **12** 4

13 10   **14** 0

15 10   **16** 210

17 200   **18** 198

19 2

20 $\frac{1}{2}$ or 0.5 or half

21 89   **22** 40

23 6   **24** 7

25 250

Paper 12

1

2   10

3 8   **4** 115

5 90   **6** 492

7 31   **8** 41

9–11 any three from: 45, 46, 47, 48, 49, 51, 52, 53, 54

12 16 ÷ 2

13 100 ÷ 10   **14** 14 ÷ 2

15 50 ÷ 5   **16** 20 ÷ 2

17 10   **18** 11

19 11   **20** 6

21 29   **22** 8

23 any two numbers with a sum of 20

24 sec   **25** hr

Paper 13

1 £4.14   **2** 81

3 44   **4** 10

5 5   **6** 50

7–9 B, D, F   **10** 63

11 62   **12** 42

13 75   **14** 70

15 6   **16** 5

17 8   **18** 3

19 8   **20** 59

21 79   **22** 186

23 161   **24** 156

25 right 1

Paper 14

1 5

2 10

3 three numbers with a sum of 10

4 7 − 6

5 15 − 8   **6** 9 − 9

7 17 − 14   **8** 80 − 65

9 60   **10** 10

11 2   **12** 70

13 16

14
5	4	6
3	5	4

15 25 + 18 = 43 or 18 + 25 = 43

16 £2 or £2.00

17 £1.10

18 £3 or £3.00

19 4

20 Rizz, Buzz, Fazz

21–25

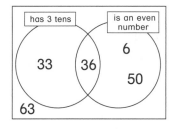

Paper 15

1 10 + 0   **2** 10 + 13

3 11 + 4   **4** 15 + 1

5 30 + 21   **6** oranges

7 plums   **8** 20

9 20   **10** 105

11 14   **12** 6

13 A = 230   **14** B = 255

15 C = 285   **16** 10

17 2   **18** 4

19 5   **20** 7

21 200 g   **22** 150 ml

23 50 min

24 $\frac{1}{2}$ m or 0.5 m or 50 cm

25 4 kg

Paper 16

1–5

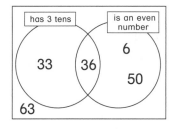

6 40

7 20   **8** 27

9 600   **10** 90

11 590   **12** 803

13 303   **14** 203

15 10   **16** 8

17 1   **18** 10

19 8   **20** 100

21 139   **22** 16

23 90   **24** 24

25 left 3

Paper 17

1 5   **2** 25

3 50   **4** 30

5 45   **6** 10

7 70   **8** 45

9 80   **10** 10

11 2   **12** 9

13 3   **14** 14

15 e.g. 6 + 4 = 20 − 10

16 8

17 3

18 4

19 6
20 9
21 e.g.

| Total 60 | Total 90 |

22 550 g
23 61 + 24 = 85
24 e.g. double 11 = 22
25 even

Paper 18

1–2

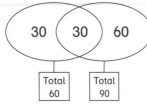

cone pyramid square cylinder cuboid triangle

3 30   **4** 10
5 95   **6** 100
7 94   **8** 11
9 4   **10** 5
11 August   **12** May
13 2   **14** 4
15 10   **16** 6
17 10   **18** 10
19 18   **20** 50
21 10   **22** 2
23 10   **24** 80
25 *accept 6 cm to 8 cm, inclusive*

Paper 19

1 5   **2** 7
3 e.g. 3 + 6 = 1 + 8
4 e.g. 6 − 0 = 7 − 1
5 e.g. 2 + 2 = 8 − 4
6 £10
7 50p or £0.50
8 £10

9 3
10 pilot, diver
11 10
12 10
13 2
14 100
15 10
16

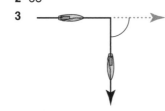

17 14   7
18 30   30
19 plane
20 bus
21 horse
22 6
23 car
24 e.g. 10 + 5 = 15
25 *accept a line 5.3 cm to 5.7 cm, inclusive*

Paper 20

1 79
2 65
3

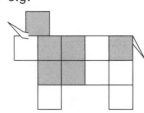

4 48
5 200
6 64
7 44
8 e.g.

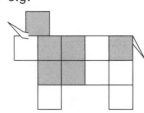

9 6
10–11 e.g. 6 × 10 = 60
          e.g. 10 × 10 = 100
12

13 e.g.

14 e.g.

15 68 − 25 = 43
16 10 × 6 = 60
17 4 × 2 = 10 − 2
18 70 + 50 = 3 × 40
19 350 ml
20 15 min
21 450 cm or 4.5 m
22 200 g
23 15 l
24 e.g.

Coins	£2	£1	50p	20p	10p
Number	3	1	3	5	4

25

A4

15 The length of a train with ten carriages

ml   g   m   l   kg   km

Write $+$, $-$ or $=$ in the circles to make the **calculations** correct.

16 17 ◯ 9 ◯ 26   **17** 50 ◯ 20 ◯ 30

18 A stool is 70 cm high.
Sebastian is 130 cm tall.

How high is Sebastian when
he stands on the stool?

19 Tom uses 75 g of a 2 kg bag of sugar.

2 kg

How many grams of sugar are
left in the bag?

20 Adam uses 125 ml of milk to make
a honey cake.

How many millilitres of milk does
he need for 10 cakes?   125 ml

21 Five children take part in a relay charity walk. Each child walks
for the same amount of time. In total they walk for one hour.

For how many minutes does each child walk?

22 Carmel makes a picture frame with two 30 cm and two 20 cm
lengths of wood.

20 cm   30 cm

What is the total length of wood she uses?

Write in the **missing numbers**.

23 $51 - 48 = 83 - \boxed{}$ **24** $73 - 67 = 92 - \boxed{}$

25 $104 - 96 = 25 - \boxed{}$

Paper 11

Write in the answers.

1 16 − 8 = ☐

2 9 − 6 = ☐

3 8 − 3 = ☐

4 10 − 8 = ☐

5 6 − 0 = ☐

6 Draw another line 5 centimetres longer than this line.

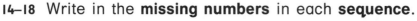

8 cm

Put a ring around the multiplication which matches the answer.

7 answer is 14 | 1 × 2 | 3 × 2 | 5 × 2 | 7 × 2 | 9 × 2 |

8 answer is 90 | 6 × 10 | 7 × 10 | 8 × 10 | 9 × 10 | 10 × 10 |

9 answer is 6 | 2 × 2 | 3 × 2 | 4 × 2 | 5 × 2 | 6 × 2 |

10 answer is 20 | 10 × 10 | 8 × 10 | 6 × 10 | 4 × 10 | 2 × 10 |

11 answer is 30 | 7 × 10 | 6 × 10 | 2 × 10 | 3 × 10 | 8 × 10 |

Write in the **missing numbers**.

12 5 + 5 + 5 + 5 = ☐ × 5

13 3 × 10 = 10 + 10 + ☐

14–18 Write in the **missing numbers** in each **sequence**.

☐ 2 4 6 8 ☐

☐ 208 206 204 202 ☐ ☐

Write in the **missing numbers**.

19 14 days = ☐ weeks   **20** 12 hours = ☐ a day   **2**

21 Anna has 79 stamps in her collection. She buys 10 more.

How many stamps does she have now? ☐

22 There are 60 houses on the estate where James lives. On the estate where Sean lives there are 20 fewer houses.

How many houses are there on Sean's estate? ☐

23 I think of a number and multiply it by 5.
The answer is 30. What was my number? ☐

24 Ramsden School takes 139 children on a school trip. Each mini-bus can hold 20 children.

What is the smallest number of mini-buses
needed for the children? ☐

25 Each day for five days a group of hens lay 70 eggs. Each day 20 of the eggs are sold.

How many eggs are left at the end of the five days? ☐   **5**

Paper 12

1 Put a ring around the box that has the most money.

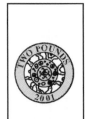   

⟨ 1

Write in the answers.

2 **half** of 20 = ⬚   3 **double** 4 = ⬚

⟨ 2

Write the numbers that are 10 less than.

4 | 125 | 10 less than is ⟶ ⬚

5 | 100 | 10 less than is ⟶ ⬚

6 | 502 | 10 less than is ⟶ ⬚

⟨ 3

Write in the answers.

7 16 + 10 + 5 = ⬚   8 23 + 8 + 10 = ⬚

⟨ 2

9–11 Write three different numbers that **round** to 50 when rounded to the nearest 10.

⬚   ⬚   ⬚

⟨ 3

In each line, put a ring around the division with the largest answer.

12 | 8 ÷ 2 | | 10 ÷ 5 | | 10 ÷ 2 | | 40 ÷ 10 | | 16 ÷ 2 |

13 | 50 ÷ 10 | | 90 ÷ 10 | | 20 ÷ 5 | | 100 ÷ 10 | | 18 ÷ 2 |

14 | 30 ÷ 10 | | 25 ÷ 5 | | 30 ÷ 5 | | 6 ÷ 2 | | 14 ÷ 2 |

15 | $50 \div 5$ | | $4 \div 2$ | | $80 \div 10$ | | $10 \div 5$ | | $2 \div 2$ |

16 | $12 \div 2$ | | $60 \div 10$ | | $40 \div 5$ | | $20 \div 2$ | | $45 \div 5$ |

This is a chart of what children in Class 2 do at lunch time.

$\bigcirc$ = 1 child

Go home

Packed lunch

School dinner

17 How many children have a school dinner?

18 How many more children have a packed lunch than go home?

19 How many fewer children go home than have a packed lunch?

20 Of those that stay for school dinner 4 are girls.

How many boys stay for school dinner?

21 How many children are in Class 2 altogether?

Write in what the **missing numbers** could be.

22 $12 + \boxed{} = 4 + 16$

23 $5 + 15 = \boxed{} + \boxed{}$

Put a ring around the best unit to measure the time it takes for:

24 a flash of lightning

   sec   min   hr   day   week

25 a train to go from London to Disneyland, Paris

   sec   min   hr   day   week

1 How much money has been left out of the money box? ⬚

2 Put a ring around the **odd number**.

92   16   70   81   44

3 What is the total of the three **even numbers**?

3   6   10   15   21   28   ⬚

Write in the answers.

4 **double** 5 = ⬚   5 **half** of 10 = ⬚

6 twice 25 = ⬚

7–9 Tick the three shaded shapes that have a **line of symmetry**.

A

B

C

D

E

F

Write in the answers.

10 $68 - 5 =$ [   ]

11 $70 - 8 =$ [   ]

12 $59 - 17 =$ [   ]

13 $85 - 10 =$ [   ]

14 $90 - 20 =$ [   ]

◯ 5

Write in the **missing numbers**.

15 $2 \times$ [   ] $= 12$

16 [   ] $\times 4 = 20$

17 $5 \times$ [   ] $= 40$

18 [   ] $\times 9 = 27$

19 $4 \times$ [   ] $= 32$

◯ 5

20–24 Write in the **missing numbers** in each **sequence**.

[   ]   63   67   71   75   [   ]

[   ]   181   176   171   166   [   ]   [   ]

◯ 5

25 Write in move 5 for the path from the mouse to the cheese.

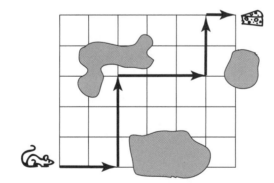

move 1:	right 2
move 2:	up 3
move 3:	right 3
move 4:	up 2
move 5:	_____

◯ 1

Paper 14

Write in what the **missing numbers** could be.

1 [   ] + 3 + 8 = 16   2 4 + [   ] + 6 = 20

3 [   ] + [   ] + [   ] = 10

3

In each line, put a ring around the subtraction that has the smallest answer.

4 | 7 − 6 | 27 − 25 | 13 − 10 | 4 − 2 | 18 − 15 |

5 | 24 − 12 | 26 − 17 | 14 − 4 | 15 − 8 | 23 − 12 |

6 | 50 − 40 | 11 − 10 | 16 − 14 | 9 − 9 | 18 − 8 |

7 | 10 − 5 | 13 − 9 | 9 − 1 | 17 − 14 | 20 − 10 |

8 | 70 − 35 | 80 − 65 | 40 − 15 | 70 − 25 | 65 − 40 |

5

Write in the answers.

9 6 × 10 = [   ]   10 5 × 2 = [   ]

11 1 × 2 = [   ]   12 7 × 10 = [   ]

13 8 × 2 = [   ]

5

14 Put rings around the three dominoes that altogether have a total of 27.

| 2 | 6 | 5 | 4 | 3 | 6 |
| 4 | 1 | 3 | 5 | 1 | 4 |

1

15 Write an addition that uses the same three numbers as the subtraction.

[43] − [18] = [25]

[   ] + [   ] = [   ]

1

Rizz
80p

Buzz
90p

Fazz
£1.20

Jezz
£1.50

16 What is the total cost of a Rizz and a Fazz?

17 Harry buys a Buzz with a £2 coin.
    How much change should he get?

18 Indira buys two Jezz ice-lollies.
    How much do they cost her altogether?

19 What is the greatest number of Fazz ice-lollies that
    can be bought with a £5 note?

20 Kylie has £3 to spend.
    Which three different ice-lollies could she buy?

    _____ and _____ and _____

5

21–25 Write the numbers 63 36 33 6 50 in the correct

places on the **Venn diagram**.

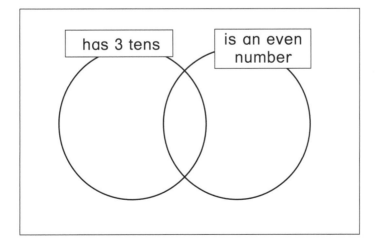

has 3 tens

is an even
number

5

Paper 15

In each line, put a ring around the addition that has the largest answer.

1	1 + 7	8 + 1	10 + 0	6 + 3	4 + 5
2	11 + 11	10 + 13	14 + 1	12 + 8	7 + 13
3	4 + 6	11 + 4	7 + 2	3 + 8	9 + 5
4	0 + 10	2 + 6	15 + 1	0 + 7	4 + 7
5	25 + 25	30 + 21	26 + 23	46 + 3	18 + 32

5

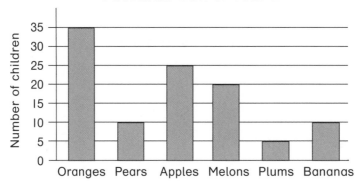

Favourite fruit of Year 2

6 Which fruit is liked best by most children? _____

7 Which fruit is liked best by the fewest children? _____

8 How many more children like apples than plums? ⬚

9 Altogether, how many children like pears and bananas? ⬚

10 How many children voted altogether? ⬚

5

Write in the answers.

11 **double** 7 = ⬚   12 **half** of 12 = ⬚

2

30

13–15 What numbers are the arrows pointing to? Write them in the boxes.

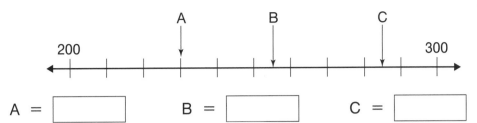

A = [＿＿＿]   B = [＿＿＿]   C = [＿＿＿]   **3**

Write in the answers.

16 20 ÷ 2 = [＿＿＿]   **17** 20 ÷ 10 = [＿＿＿]

18 8 ÷ 2 = [＿＿＿]   **19** 50 ÷ 10 = [＿＿＿]

20 14 ÷ 2 = [＿＿＿]   **5**

21 Nyla weighs 150 g of flour. She puts another 50 g
on the scales.

How much flour has she weighed altogether?   [＿＿＿]

22 Ricky buys a 250 ml can of cola.
He drinks 100 ml.

How much is left in Ricky's can?   [＿＿＿]

23 On a journey a train stops for five minutes at
every station.

It stops at ten stations altogether.

What is the total time the train stops at the stations?   [＿＿＿]

24 Shahid saws a one metre length of wood into
two equal lengths.

What is the length of one piece?   [＿＿＿]

25 Amy buys five 2 kg bags of apples. She uses
6 kg of the apples to bake apple pies.

How many kilograms of apples are left?   [＿＿＿]   **5**

Paper 16

1–5 Draw lines to match the times.

| 12:15 | 6:00 | 3:15 | 9:45 | 9:30 |

Write in the **missing numbers**.

6 [　　　] + 30 = 70 　　　　7 80 + [　　　] = 100

8 [　　　] + 20 = 47 　　　　9 300 + [　　　] = 900

10–14 Write in the **missing numbers** in each **sequence**.

[　　　]　190　290　390　490　[　　　]

[　　　]　703　603　503　403　[　　　]　[　　　]

Put a ring around the correct **missing number**.

15　10 ÷ [　　　] = 1　　| 1　2　3　4　5　6　7　8　9　10 |

16　[　　　] ÷ 2 = 4　　| 1　2　3　4　5　6　7　8　9　10 |

17　3 ÷ [　　　] = 3　　| 1　2　3　4　5　6　7　8　9　10 |

18　100 ÷ [　　　] = 10　| 1　2　3　4　5　6　7　8　9　10 |

19　[　　　] ÷ 1 = 8　　| 1　2　3　4　5　6　7　8　9　10 |

20 In a game of skittles Caitlin scores 80 points and then a further 20 points.

How many points does she score altogether?

21 A shop has 189 bars of ice-cream. It sells 50 of them.

How many bars of ice-cream does it have left?

22 Jodie has two fish tanks with eight fish in each tank.

How many fish does Jodie have altogether?

23 I think of a number and divide it by 10. The answer is 9.

What was my number?

24 Beth has 24 swap cards. She buys another 24 swap cards and then shares all her cards equally between herself and her brother.

How many cards does each of them get?

5

25 Write in the missing move 4 for the path from the spider to the fly.

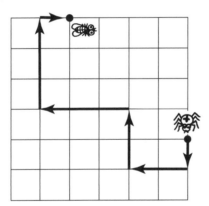

move 1:	down 1
move 2:	left 2
move 3:	up 2
move 4:	_____
move 5:	up 3
move 6:	right 1

1

Paper 17

Write in the answers.

1 $1 \times 5 =$ ⬚

2 $5 \times 5 =$ ⬚

3 $10 \times 5 =$ ⬚

4 $6 \times 5 =$ ⬚

5 $9 \times 5 =$ ⬚

○ 5

Write in the answers.

6 **half** of 20 = ⬚

7 **double** 35 = ⬚

8 **half** of 90 = ⬚

○ 3

10 small spoonfuls = 1 large spoonful

9 How many small spoonfuls will fill 8 large spoons? ⬚

10 How many large spoonfuls are needed to fill 100 small spoons? ⬚

○ 2

Write in what the **missing numbers** could be.

11 $9 -$ ⬚ $= 7 + 0$

12 $6 - 5 = 10 -$ ⬚

13 $8 -$ ⬚ $= 7 - 2$

14 ⬚ $- 7 = 4 + 3$

15 $6 +$ ⬚ $= 20 -$ ⬚

○ 5

Put a ring around the correct answers.

16 $16 \div 2 =$ | 1 2 3 4 5 6 7 8 9 10 |

17 $6 \div 2 =$ | 1 2 3 4 5 6 7 8 9 10 |

18 $40 \div 10 =$ | 1 2 3 4 5 6 7 8 9 10 |

19 60 ÷ 10 = | 1   2   3   4   5   6   7   8   9   10 |

20 90 ÷ 10 = | 1   2   3   4   5   6   7   8   9   10 |

○ 5

21 Write three numbers in the two ovals to make the totals in each oval.

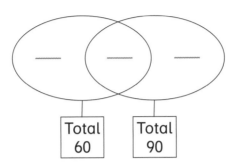

Total 60   Total 90

○ 1

22 What is the weight of the parcel?

○ 1

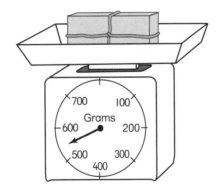

700   100
Grams
600   200
500   300
400

23 Work out the missing **digits** so the **calculation** is correct.

| | 1 | + | 2 | | = | 8 | 5 |

○ 1

24–25 Saul says,

"When you double an odd number the answer is an even number."

Write in two numbers to match what Saul says.

Double [   ] = [   ]

Is your answer an **even** or an **odd number**? _____

○ 2

Now go to the Progress Chart to record your score!   Total ○ 25

Paper 18

1–2 Match the drawing of each 3-D shape to its name.

cone   pyramid   square   cylinder   cuboid   triangle

2

Write in the **missing numbers**.

3   50 + 50 = ☐ + 70

4   90 + ☐ = 60 + 40

2

5   Put a ring around the **multiple** of 5.

    52   41   87   95   56

6   Put a ring around the **multiple** of 10.

    442   217   100   203   304

7   Put a ring around the **multiple** of 2.

    25   129   91   87   94

3

8   How many tens make 110? ☐

1

Write in the **missing numbers**.

9   10 ÷ 5 = 8 ÷ ☐   10   20 ÷ 2 = 2 × ☐

2

36

11 Which month comes immediately after July? _____

12 Which month comes seven months
before December? _____ **2**

Put a ring around the correct **missing number**.

13 $9 \times$ [ ] $= 18$ | 1   2   3   4   5   6   7   8   9   10

14 [ ] $\times 10 = 40$ | 1   2   3   4   5   6   7   8   9   10

15 $10 \times$ [ ] $= 100$ | 1   2   3   4   5   6   7   8   9   10

16 [ ] $\times 2 = 12$ | 1   2   3   4   5   6   7   8   9   10

17 $8 \times$ [ ] $= 80$ | 1   2   3   4   5   6   7   8   9   10 **5**

Write in the **missing numbers**.

18 double [ ] $= 20$ **19 half** of [ ] $= 9$ **2**

Write in the **missing numbers**.

20 [ ] $\div 2 = 25$ **21** $20 \div$ [ ] $= 2$

22 $90 \div$ [ ] $= 45$ **23** [ ] $\div 1 = 10$

24 [ ] $\div 10 = 8$ **5**

25 This line is 1 cm long.

  1 cm
  |—————|

Estimate in centimetres the distance around the
outside of the wheel. [ ] **1**

Paper 19

Write in what the **missing numbers** could be.

1 5 + [ ] = 8 + 2

2 [ ] + 2 = 9 + 0

3 3 + [ ] = 1 + [ ]

4 [ ] − 0 = [ ] − 1

5 [ ] + [ ] = 8 − 4

Fireman	Policewoman	Pilot	Diver
£2	£3	£1.50	£5

6 What is the total cost of a fireman, a policewoman and a diver? [ ]

7 Bryn has £4.50.
How much more does he need to buy a diver? [ ]

8 What is the total cost of five firemen? [ ]

9 How many policewomen can be bought with a £10 note? [ ]

10 Sally has £7 to spend.
Which two toys does she buy if she is given 50p change?

_____ and _____

Write in the **missing numbers**.

11 [ ] ÷ 2 = 5

12 70 ÷ [ ] = 7

13 18 ÷ [ ] = 9

14 [ ] ÷ 10 = 10

15 80 ÷ [ ] = 8

16 Shade the correct part of the circle after the turn.

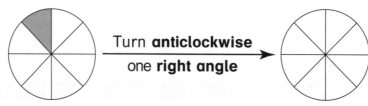

Turn **anticlockwise** one **right angle**

Write in the **missing numbers**.

17 [ ] —— **halve** ——> [ ] —— **double** ——> | 14 |

18 [ ] —— **double** ——> | 60 | —— **halve** ——> [ ]

○ 2

Favourite types of transport

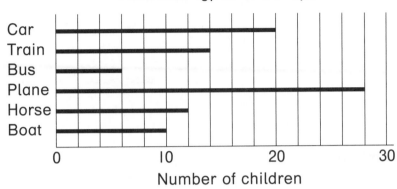

Number of children

19 Which type of transport is the favourite of most children?

_____

20 Which is the least favourite type of transport?   _____

21 Which type of transport is liked best by
exactly 12 children?   _____

22 How many more children like cars than trains best?   [   ]

23 Which type of transport is liked best by twice as
many as those who like boats best?   _____

○ 5

24 Becky says, "*When you add two numbers that divide exactly by
5 the answer divides exactly by 10.*"

Write an example to show that what Becky says is not always true.

[   ] + [   ] = [   ]

○ 1

25 Draw another line that is **half** the length of this line.

_____

○ 1

Paper 20

Write in the **missing numbers**.

1 82 − [ ] = 3   2 [ ] − 58 = 7   **2**

3 Tick the boat that has turned through a **right angle**.

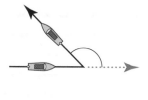

Write in the **missing numbers**.

4 [ ] − 30 = 18   5 700 − [ ] = 500

6 [ ] − 21 = 43   7 98 − [ ] = 54   **4**

8 Three squares of the animal are shaded. Shade more squares so that **half** of the animal is shaded.

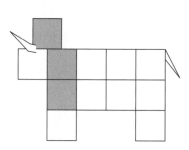

9 What is $\frac{1}{2}$ of 12?   [ ]   **1**

Fazir says,

"Every number in the ten times table ends in 0."

Write two examples to show what Fazir means.

10 [ ] × [10] = [ ]

11 [ ] × [10] = [ ]   **2**

(40)

Draw more lines to make each shape.

12

Complete the triangle.

13

Complete a **quadrilateral**.

14

Complete a **pentagon**.

○ 3

15 Write in the missing **digits**.

$$\boxed{6\ \ \square} - \boxed{\square\ \ 5} = \boxed{4\ \ 3}$$

○ 1

Write +, −, × or = in the circles to make each of the **calculations** correct.

16 10 ○ 6 ○ 60

17 4 ○ 2 ○ 10 ○ 2

18 70 ○ 50 ○ 3 ○ 40

○ 3

19 Adele puts 200 ml of milk into a jug. She then puts another 150 ml into the jug.
How much milk is in the jug now?

20 Natasha left school at a quarter-past three.
She got home at half-past three.
How many minutes did it take Natasha to get home?

21 A kerbstone is 90 cm long.
What is the total length of five kerbstones?

22 Chumo's mum buys 1 kg of sweets. She shares them equally between five children.
How many grams of sweets does each child get?

23 For a party Perry's dad uses three 1 litre bottles of apple juice.

He mixes each bottle with 4 litres of fizzy water.

How many litres of apple drink does he make?

○ 5

24

Coins	£2	£1	50p	20p	10p
Number					

Simon has £9.90 in £2, £1, 50p, 20p and 10p coins.

Write in the table the number of each coin that he could have.

25 Shade the square after the turn.

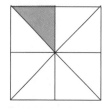

Turn **clockwise**
$\frac{3}{4}$ of a whole turn

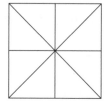

Progress Chart   Maths 6-7 years

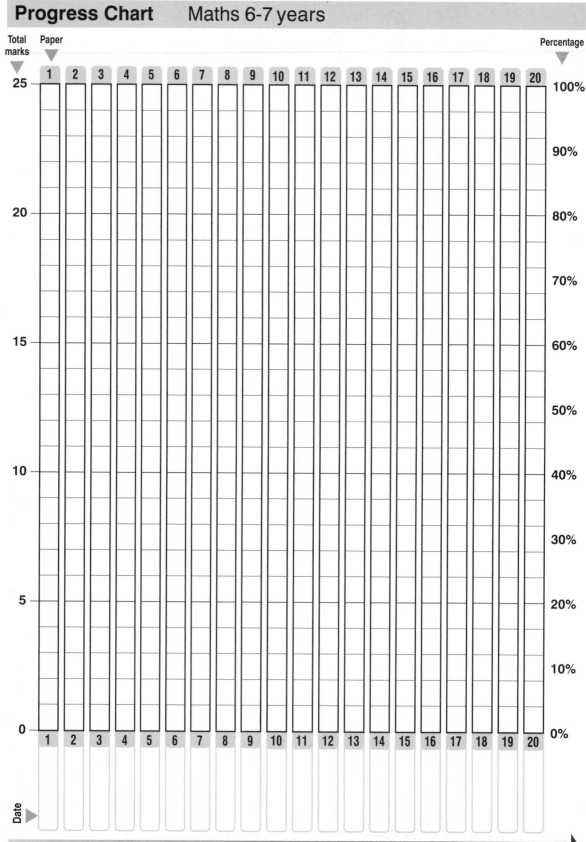

Total marks

Paper

Percentage

25 — 100%

90%

20 — 80%

70%

15 — 60%

50%

10 — 40%

30%

5 — 20%

10%

0 — 0%

Paper: 1 2 3 4 5 6 7 8 9 10 11 12 13 14 15 16 17 18 19 20

Date

When you've finished the book read the Next Steps